GROWING in FAITH

Skyping with **God** on a daily basis

Joys Priscilla Oyedepo

GROWING IN FAITH
Copyright © 2018 by:
Joys Priscilla Oyedepo
ISBN 978-2480-44-4

Published in Nigeria by:
DOMINION PUBLISHING HOUSE

All rights reserved.
No portion of this book may be used without the written permission of the publisher, with the exception of brief excerpts in magazines, articles, reviews, etc.

Dominion Publishing House is an affiliate of the Christian organization, **Living Faith Church Worldwide a.k.a Winners' Chapel International**. We will in no way endorse or publish any material considered controversial, immoral or against the Christian Faith.

For further information or permission, address:

DOMINION PUBLISHING HOUSE
Km 10, Idiroko Road, Canaanland, Ota, Nigeria.
Tel: +234 816 406 0777, +234 909 151 4022

Or visit our website: ***www.dphprints.com***

Connect with Joys Priscilla Oyedepo

- Joys Priscilla Oyedepo
- @JoysOyedepo
- @JoysOyedepo
- www.JoysOyedepo.com

All Bible Quotes in NLT except otherwise stated.

Table of Contents

Dedication	5
Introduction	7
1. Our Relationship With Christ	9
2. Why Don't I See The Acts Of God Through My Hands?	19
3. Unattractive Obedience	29
4. Idolatry In Today's World	37
5. Sustaining Our Virginity In Christ	47
6. Does Judgement Day Scare You?	57
7. Coloured Friendships	65
8. Your Friends Know Who You Are	73
9. The Sickle Of Competition	83
10. What Your Eyes See And Ears Hear	93
11. Through The Noise	103
12. The Lesser Job	108
13. Faith Positioning	123
Salvation Prayer	135

Dedication

This book is dedicated to all who are pursuing the heart of God daily;

striving to silence all the distractions on their path.

Introduction

As young women in today's generation, we get so caught up in the *works* of everyday life. We worry about being in that relationship that would be Instagram-worthy; about what jobs would satisfy us, what our friends think about us, what it would take to get the *hottest* clothes off of the runway or the most expensive *red-bottom Louboutins* for the cheapest price. For the most part, we *forget* that our relationship with God is the most important of all.

In Genesis 1:27, the Bible says,

> *"So God created human beings in his own image. In the image of God he created* **them;** *male and* **female** *he created them."*

At creation, God brought man and woman to being. He created **all** males and females in that instant—interestingly enough, even when Adam was the only human roaming the earth. It is not until Genesis

2:22 that "Eve" was made from Adam's ribs; but from Chapter 1:27, she had been *created*.

God is a humorous God. He knows the end from the beginning. This is why He says in Jeremiah 29:11, "…**I know** the plans I have for you." He knows what it is that He has in store for you and so, He confidently goes on to say in that same verse of scripture that, "They are plans for good and not for disaster, to give you a future and a hope." What an awesome God we serve!

God knew where you would be today and He knew that you would need this book to put you in *check,* and to bring you closer to His heart. So, He has put this in your hands. Read this book with all intent therefore, and watch as your relationship with God goes from glory to greater glory!

Get set for a life changing encounter!

1
Our Relationship With Christ

Recently, I began thinking on what it means to have a relationship with Christ. As a Christian woman living, working, eating, breathing, in a church, Christ-centred environment on a daily basis, it is so easy to think of this relationship with Christ as nothing but the *norm*. We see it as a norm that needs not to be developed and so our crave for more of God either decreases or remains the same.

On the other hand, and in today's *social* world however, a relationship with Christ has been *modernised* to mean solely *associating with Christianity*. The four-walled glass screen of a global village show us the many

The four-walled glass screen of a global village show us the many women that claim an Instagram bio of Christianity but a display picture of the private goods of all their woman, leaving nothing to the imagination of their sheer nakedness.

women that claim an Instagram *bio* of Christianity but a *display picture* of the *private goods* of all their woman, leaving nothing to the imagination of their sheer nakedness. Even beyond that, many sing songs of redemption, claim dates of salvation, shout and clap hands weekly in His sanctuary, but are far away from His heart. I mean, many even claim trust in *modern day revivals only—no old school stuff*; and all of this is only but a miniscule portion of what Christianity has been turned to today. The world pushes out Christ from the *—ianity* and then encourages its idols become our lifestyle and *religion*. This is why today, more than ever before, a true relationship with Christ is critical for every believer.

In October of 2015, God began working on my heart regarding this relationship with Him—my relationship with Him. He made it clear that it was a relationship based off of a growing knowledge of His truth **and** faith. It was never about *total* understanding of His person prior to this belief, as if it was the case, this relationship would not be called *the faith* but *the understanding.* As a result, in my daily devotions, my heart's *cry* was to grow in my trust of Him, more than in a *complete* understanding of Him prior to this trust.

With reckless abandon and in the same month, God then led me to officially launch *Women Of The God*

Kind. It was the start of a move that was very much needed; but I knew that I dare not step out before the clear directives of *Abba*. Within only a few days of its launch, I received messages from several women asking, "Am I a *Woman Of The God Kind*?" or "I wear short skirts and holler and scream at my favourite clubs on a Friday night but I still love God so I must also be #WOTGK! Right?"

These questions may have been worded differently but my response to such questions, whether in person or via email and/or social media were pretty consistent. It goes something like this: "Sweetie, I don't know. All I can see are your works but God sees your heart. The essence of *Women Of The God Kind* is to put us in check; to teach and train us, until we become women that operate on the same frequency as God."

Well, "is that possible?" you may ask; or maybe your question is, "isn't that *blasphemy*—to operate on **His** frequency?"

Well, John 14: 12 (NIV) says,

> **"Very truly I tell you, whoever believes in me will do the works I have been doing, and they will do even greater things *than these*, because I am going to the Father."**

Jesus says that as long as we believe in Him, we are

capable of doing even greater works than He did while on this earth! Isn't that amazing?! We have been blessed enough to do such great works—all because we believe **in Him**!

Did Christ heal the sick (Acts 10:38)? Then, you can do it too!

Did He raise the dead (Mark 5:41)? Then, YOU can do it too!

Yes, YOU TOO can lay hands on the sick and they will recover! You **should** lay hands on the sick and see them recover—it is a commandment!

In Mark 16:18, we see that the last 11 words that Jesus spoke while still physically on this earth. He said,

"...[you] **shall** lay hands on the sick, and they shall recover." (NLT)

He said this concerning the *believers* and so as long as you and I believe *in* Him, we should lay hands on the sick—and see them recover!

When God started opening my eyes to this, He led me to two people—a man and a woman—who would teach me the rudiments of healing. They had gone to be with the Lord and so the Lord told me that I would sit under their teachings through their videos and books. I was so excited and began watching their videos daily. During that season, I truly saw God work in and through me like *never* before.

I had learnt how to *realign* the human pelvic region by the power of God's Holy Spirit (for any persons with waist pains, etc.) and later on that Saturday, I was at a fellowship. I had been fasting that day and suddenly, during prayers, I had this acute and intense waist pain. I had the option to step out and try to figure out what was wrong (but remain in same pain), or *to heal myself*—through the power of the same Holy Spirit I had been so vigorously learning about.

I thought, "this is exciting! God is giving me good practice!" So, I stood up, said a 15 second or less prayer, and I saw God work! Goodness—my pelvis was physically rotating! I wasn't moving my waist—it was moving itself and I was in total awe of God! With such a large number of people in the room, I couldn't scream, I couldn't cry (although, almost did!); but I could give Him glory! I waited for the alignment to be complete and for the movement to stop. Immediately it stopped, I called out a sister-friend of mine to the corridor— I had to share the *good* news! The healing power of God is real, can be taught, and can work through our very own *hands*!

As we had been going to hospitals on the weekends to pray for patients during this season, I got even more excited! The Saturday that followed, we met with a man at the hospital who had a strange illness. He had been connected to a catheter because he couldn't even stand up to use the bathroom! He had no appetite and so was completely weak; then, he also had become completely paralyzed in his legs. I was excited to pray for him. I asked him what he wanted healed (as I usually do—although sometimes, they say *all* things—and that's what I pray for). This time, he could barely speak but whispered that he wanted his appetite back. I asked a man also in our group to place his hand on his appestat and I prayed a restored appetite. I told him to get ready to get hungry, and then we went to the next ward. Barely five minutes later, I saw his daughter run out to wash an empty bowl. When I asked her what had happened, she said that he had finished a bowl of *pap* (a popular semi-liquid food in Nigeria). For the first time since he had the strange illness come upon him, his appetite was back—he was healed! In the same hospital, I also saw many others that I prayed for, get healed. Those with iron casts in their thighs and feet got healed and in barely hours to days, the casts had to be removed and they were discharged. I mean, divine healings of all kinds; and it's the same anointing that we all have, once we have the Holy Spirit.

So, the question is, if we have this power, why aren't we all aware and/or using it?

First of all and before I go any deeper, it is important that we understand that **merely seeing signs and wonders are no guarantee that it is God at work**. In these *end times*, there will be many who will perform signs and wonders—but *not* in the name of the Lord. In Revelation 13:14, John, still telling of this mighty vision said,

> *"And with* **all the miracles he was allowed to perform on behalf of the first beast,** *he* **deceived** *all the people who belong to this world.* **He ordered the people to make a great statue of the first beast,** *who was fatally wounded and then came back to life."*

I mean, my goodness, a *beast* performing miracles and then by so doing leading more to the devil! "Miracles?" you may ask; "why, how?"

[**Please Note:** I encourage you to read the Bible Book of Revelation. It will open your eyes to so much truth and WILL lead you closer to the heart of the Father. You will truly understand why the Bible says that of all that were born of women, none was as great as John—**until now**. By seeing and understanding the relationship John the Baptist had with God, you and I can know the core of what to crave for.]

The devil will try to pretend to be *of God*, so as to

...merely seeing signs and wonders are no guarantee that it is God at work.

mislead masses, to himself. He will create counterfeit acts; but only God creates true acts. How can you know the difference?

-With the help of the Holy Spirit.

As soon as you have God, you must hold Him close. Like Jacob, we must say, "I will NOT let you go!"

The Holy Spirit is our guide—He tells us right from wrong and convicts our heart of sin, unrighteousness and *worldliness*. If we do not have the Holy Spirit alive and working within us therefore, we need to ensure that we do—now!

So, if you don't yet have Him alive in your heart **with the evidence of speaking in tongues, drop this book right now**. Go before Him and ask Him to come into your heart.

Separate yourself—so, if you are in the midst of people reading this book, leave them *all*. Go into a closet, a bathroom—wherever you can be secluded—and cry out to Him. Give Him absolutely **nothing less than 15 minutes**—and **mean it**!

The Holy Spirit now is welcome into your heart.

2

Why Don't I See The Acts Of God Through My Hands?

For the most part, I have found that as Christians, one major reason why we don't see the acts of God in and through us is because we stay the *same* and don't aspire to grow, in Him. We don't work on building ourselves or growing. As physical beings, we grow—so why shouldn't we ensure that we grow our spirit beings as well?

Take for example a little girl. At the age of 1 she says her first word… "daada!" Her parents are so excited and her father is most excited because well, she called him first! How wonderful.

As physical beings,

we grow—so why

shouldn't we ensure

that we grow our

spirit beings as well?

Now, imagine that the same girl at 24 years old, still saying only one word—"daada!" That is, she's physically grown; and now at 24 and maybe 5 feet 10 inches tall, she can speak nothing but that one word.

Would her parents be worried? Absolutely! Would her friends be worried? I mean, if she can make any— absolutely! Would you, even if merely a neighbour or just a concerned acquaintance who finds out about her situation be worried? I would think so! All because she is expected to have grown—mentally and cognitively, not just physically; so there would be *natural* reasons to worry.

In the same vein, anyone who grows physically (in height, weight, beauty, etc.) should strive to grow spiritually so as not to be deemed a deformed personality— in the realm of the Spirit.

Some say, "well, that makes no sense. There is nothing like a spirit realm" or "prove to me that there is a spiritual realm then I'll work on building it." So, for that reason, let me explain it way:

Do you know where your **mind** is?

NOTE: Not your brain but your <u>mind</u>.

We've had scientists speculate on where the mind is, for generations and generations. There still isn't an answer to where exactly it is in us as humans. Yet we go to school, read books, scout websites and have intelligent conversations to build this *mind* of ours.

So, the argument that we do not know where our spirit is and therefore don't have to feed it is invalid. The spirit is just as present as the mind is. Just because we cannot see it doesn't mean it doesn't exist.

When I think on my relationship with God, it makes me truly excited.

Matthew 25:1-13 tells us the parable of the ten bridesmaids. This parable has many significances but let's begin by first, reading it.

> [1]*"Then the Kingdom of Heaven will be like ten bridesmaids who took their lamps and went to meet the bridegroom. [2]Five of them were foolish, and five were wise. [3]The five who were foolish didn't take enough olive oil for their lamps, [4]but the other five were wise enough to take along extra oil. [5]When the bridegroom was delayed, they all became drowsy and fell asleep.*
>
> [6]*"At midnight they were roused by the shout, 'Look, the bridegroom is coming! Come out and meet him!'*
>
> [7]*"All the bridesmaids got up and prepared their lamps. [8]Then the five foolish ones asked the others, 'Please give us some of your oil because our lamps are going out.'*

The spirit is just as
present as the mind is.
Just because we cannot
see it doesn't mean it
doesn't exist.

> *⁹"But the others replied, 'We don't have enough for all of us. Go to a shop and buy some for yourselves.'*
>
> *¹⁰"But while they were gone to buy oil, the bridegroom came. Then those who were ready went in with him to the marriage feast, and the door was locked. ¹¹Later, when the other five bridesmaids returned, they stood outside, calling, 'Lord! Lord! Open the door for us!'*
>
> *¹²"But he called back, 'Believe me, I don't know you!'*
>
> *¹³"So you, too, must keep watch! For you do not know the day or hour of my return."*

Have you ever imagined the bond between a new bride and her groom?

If you are married now, the bond you so wished for—and hopefully do have; and if you're not yet married, the bond you pray to have?

A bride is always excited on her wedding day.

Now imagine that this bride loves her husband very much but has to leave him for a long period of time for her job. Imagine the hope and desire she has for the day she will be reunited with him!

This is the exact same thing with you, once you are born again, and Christ.

You are His bride and He is your *Groom*.

Oh, how I love to imagine this.

You know how that any bride in this situation who loves her groom would anticipate the early mornings and late nights that she can talk with her husband? Whether it is over the phone, via *Skype* or *Facetime*, she waits for the moment that she gets to hear his voice and see his *handsome* face again. Everything about him seems so perfect, and so she wants him to be her last sigh of relief before she goes to bed.

These beautiful moments of anticipation, building up to talk time that may only last a few minutes at a time with her groom, is what our relationship with God should be.

Christ is our Bride*groom* and He sent us down to this earth as His representatives (and also so we can see a part of who He was and how He lived while on this earth—what a privilege)!

If we truly love Him as much as we say we do then, we wouldn't be able to hold ourselves throughout the day because we would be waiting for the time we get to *Skype* with Him at night. We would be taking work breaks just to chit-chat with Him and tell Him how much we love, miss and can't wait to see Him (on that last day)! We would ever so often ask to *Skype* through the night with Him in visions, dreams, and sweet memories. We would want to spend every passing moment with Him—anticipating when we would be reunited. That's the power of *true* love—the kind of love that lasts a lifetime and will swim the seven seas and climb the highest mountains. This is the kind of love that would die on the cross—filled with pain and agony—for mine and your sake. The kind of love that **did** die on the cross—filled with pain and agony—for mine and your sake.

Only when we build this intimate relationship with our Bride*groom*, will He dwell so heavily with us, that we would be known with and for each other.

You know, the new bride would be at the office sending love messages to her groom at odd hours, and even during meetings. She would Skype him even when she works at an *open* desk. When the girls go to chit-chat in the bathroom, that's who she's talking about. When it's time for a workers dinner, that's who she's bringing with her; and when she has plans with him, that's when she cancels any and every other event that may try to ruin that—even when it has to do with her day job.

Truth is, after a while, everyone starts to recognize her with her groom. Her friends begin to ask about him because they know that it is the best way to get her attention. They begin to care because she cares so much.

If he's a watch maker, he begins to give her the best watches. If he's a clothing designer, she starts to flaunt his designs. If he's a professional pilot, best believe he's snuck her on some amazing flights. She not only becomes his representative willingly; he wants her to be the better reflection of the man that he is. He wants everyone to know that he takes care of *his woman*; and if he's good, he wants her not only to think that he's great, but also that he is the greatest, for her. She becomes his showpiece.

In the same vein, when we love on our Bridegroom and make all of who we are associated with Him and His work, He makes sure that we become the embodiment of all that He is. When we make Him our priority, He sneaks us into the most amazing places, giving us many times, undue access to the secret VIP rooms of the Heavens. He shows us things that the world has never seen, and makes us His showpiece.

Only at this point, would we become true vessels of His power, and carriers of His anointing. Only when we are known with Him and He is known with us, would He delightfully make Himself known through us. This is the key, if we must see the acts of God made manifest, through our hands.

When we make Him our priority, He sneaks us into the most amazing places, giving us many times, undue access to the secret VIP rooms of the Heavens.

3

Unattractive Obedience

We just talked about this beautiful, loving relationship between us and our Bridegroom, Jesus Christ. However, m*any* times, obedience to God is unattractive. It isn't *cool* nor is it what you should do when you want to be a part of this *cool* crowd. I mean, every guy was going on their merry way, having *fun* sinning against God and then here comes this man who says that God spoke to Him to build an ark; an ark that would save only those on board from total destruction. *Crazy*, right? I mean, *who thinks like that?!*, the seemingly *sane* would say.

Or, think about when Abraham came to tell members of his household that all the males would be circumcised. First, he's 99 years old and he says that he heard from

God to do this? I am so sure that some of the males would have thought to themselves, "this man is crazy! I'm sure he didn't hear from this God. He's probably just getting too old now and is seeing things; but... he's our father/boss so we've got to do it." I'm pretty sure that some would have even prayed to God to "heal this man of his stupidity!"

However, amidst such great *unattractiveness*, the men obeyed—and their obedience paid off. Today we all sing songs proclaiming how blessed we are to be daughters of Abraham. Think for a second—though seemingly greatly unattractive, obedience to God brings forth amazing results.

Now, how many times has God told you to do something?

Maybe nothing as extreme as giving away everything you own or moving to a country where you know no one just to start a ministry but little things like spending time with Him in the mornings. How many times have you had those reoccurring dreams of rapture in which you pray to God sobbing and saying, "Lord, just give me this one more chance—I promise, I will spend one hour with you every morning! Lord, **I promise!**" Well, He gives you yet another opportunity to wake up and see a beautiful day but instead of spending that one hour you promised with Him, you say a few words in prayer out of fear and five minutes later, you're on *Instagram*—judging pictures that really, are none of your business in the first place.

Thing is, God wants your heart. He wants your worries, your fears, your love, your time, your **heart**.

He has everything He will *ever* need but much more, he *wants* more time with **you**.

Do you understand what it is you just read?

... God wants more time with you!

Who are we as mere mortals that He would care so much for us (Psalm 8:4)?—but He does!

He wants you to wake up every morning and crave time with Him. He wants you to desire to *Skype* with Him as your bride*groom*. God wants His bride to miss Him as much as He misses her. He wants your time together to be the best part of your days—the most desired part of your days. God ALMIGHTY—the One Who can have whoever He wants, however He wants, at whatever time He wants, is asking just to spend some more time with **you**!

Would you honour Him?

You may be thinking, what would make a man believe God to the point of enduring consistent mockery from the world without wavering? Well, the answer is *quite* simple.

The key is in being completely *sold out* to God.

Obedience is costly and unattractive. It may initially repel society from you but the more you follow through on the same, the more you attract God to yourself; attracting more of His favours and blessings.

I am reminded of the story of my parents.

My father was greatly mocked for being a Christian who laid down everything he had and was, at the altar of Christ. If an opportunity to teach the gospel came up, he chose that over anything else. At a time and in a place where this kind of behaviour was synonymous with *stupidity*, he was heavily mocked as a *Jesus freak*! If only *they* knew that being a Jesus freak meant **greatness**! My mother stuck by Him as they built on this relationship with God, together.

The more they were mocked, the higher God took them. As a result, today, I am so blessed to truly understand the impact of obedience merely by looking into their eyes, daily. To follow the *greatness* God guarantees God-greatness in and through the life of any (wo)man.

Would you lose *friends* following Jesus? Almost definitely! Would you be mocked? Oh, absolutely! Would you think of quitting your obedience journey some nights, crying some nights or reassessing what

Obedience is costly
and unattractive.

God said to fit popular opinion? Most probably.

BUT you **MUST** remain focused.

If Abraham decided that he didn't want to look *too crazy* and so wouldn't go ahead to circumcise himself and his household, would we still be just as joyful today singing about being the seed of Abraham? Maybe not.

Sweet friend, do not bother yourself about whatever it is they say about you. You must be determined to press through. If it means staying off of social media, do it. If it means giving up your phone for a couple weeks, do it—but do NOT let anything or anyone, deter you from God.

On the day that the *Women Of The God Kind* website was to launch, I remember sitting in the service as my mother ministered and then flipping to Isaiah 51:7. The Scripture was not mentioned in the service but I distinctly remember being divinely directed to it and I want to share it with you. It says,

"Listen to me, you who know right from wrong, you who cherish my law in your hearts. Do not be afraid of people's scorn, nor fear their insults."

How powerful!

I recommend that we all read through Isaiah 51.

I mean, the Word of God is so true.

You are a Heaven
alien on this earth...
a special breed.

If you are following the ways of God, the Bible says that you are on the strait and narrow way (Matthew 7:14)! That same scripture says that only **few** find it. Only **few** will find it.

Sweetie, you are not a part of their statistic. You are not of this world, you merely live in it. You are a part of the few and so, you are on assignment on this earth to create paths. You are a Heaven alien on this earth... a special breed; so, **you must not limit yourself to being merely another clay vessel, running around controlled by sin.**

You were created special—a part of the heavenly breed ordained to produce divine results; as you follow *strict* orders. So don't be moved by their insults. **Earthen vessels just cannot understand Heavenly operations!**

Remember, it may seem so unattractive serving God but the results are priceless!

What an awesome God we serve.

4

Idolatry In Today's World

As we read above from Matthew 25:1-10, the Bridegroom is coming; and it will be at a time when we least expect it. The more I read the Book of Revelation, the more I understand that every single one of us is given more than a fair chance at repentance. God gives us multiple chances, proclaiming at most partial judgments, until His cup of wrath is full.

Why?

Why wouldn't He just give His complete judgment at once? Anyone who doesn't receive Him after the first or second time has made up their mind and so would never serve Him, right? I mean, if God is giving these chances over and over again, then why aren't the people repenting? Why isn't there a stampede of men and women rushing toward His altar throughout that Book; rather, men and women still cursing Him? We may say to ourselves, "oh, that could never be me. I know that if God gives me a second chance, I would surrender. All I want is that He'll let me know right before the rapture."

Sweets, first of all, He's letting you know right now and this is before the rapture. He's given you **this book** and led you through to this page to let you know that He is coming sooner than you think and He wants you in His camp. He wants you seated in the Heavens but you must be *clean*. You cannot be stained by this world yet expect to enter Heaven—that would never work; so, you must repent **now**.

Secondly, don't you think that many of those who God talks about throughout the Book of Revelation that curse at Him without fail were once in your position saying, "Oh, I would never! I could never curse God!" Don't you know that some who are no longer in the Faith today once lived joyfully for Christ but then let sin get in the way of that relationship?

I have learnt that once you give into temptation, no matter how *small*, you begin to sin; and the more you sin, the farther back *you push yourself* from God.

Note that I say, **YOU push *yourself*.**

This is because God is not the One pushing you away

God is not the One
pushing you away
from Himself.

from Himself. He is hoping so deeply, that you would run into His arms—and He's big, strong, and powerful enough to catch you. Yes, you may have sinned—maybe even numerous times in areas that make you feel like your soul in itself is dirt; but do NOT believe the lies of the enemy. The devil will say to you that you are too stained for God to love so you might as well keep sinning. God says though that, "I'm the stain remover! I'm not as excited about the *clean* clothes as I am, the *dirty*!"

Think on your washing detergents. I can just imagine in my mind a cap of liquid *washing detergent* being poured into a large bowl of stained clothes. Any detergent would be so much happier washing off the stains from that load of dirty laundry than from a load of laundry that is relatively all white, clean and neat. Why? Well, because it gets praised only when the stains that it cleans are clearly visible. This is why washing detergent commercials tend to show a dirty cloth first and then what it should look like when you use their detergent. They don't show you a crisp white cloth first and then the same cloth after using the detergent because you won't be able to see the cleaning power of that detergent. **Oh, what a joy that Jesus Christ, the Lamb and washing detergent of all souls is here to wash you clean and make you white as snow.** Glory to Jesus!

So, don't let the devil tempt you into running away from the heart of the Father; run so strongly towards Him instead.

A young lady once shared with me her story. She lost her father at an early age and so very early on, she began seeking for love and attention from other men. It began from what seemed like the *small* things—a hug here and there, to flirting with literally *everything* that moved, to kissing them, doing everything but sex and then finally, sex. She was to the point that she had had sex with man after man but almost always got left to the side. This consistently made her feel rejected but again, instead of running to God, she kept running to sex. She wanted to stop but felt those sexual desires were bigger than her will and strength to resist. With this, she intentionally began running farther away from God (which is what the devil wanted); but God gave her absolutely no rest. He appeared to her in dreams, spoke to her through others, and answered her late night prayers which she made consistently with tears in her eyes. Did the devil want her to be set free? Absolutely not! But God was determined and as always, He won the battle.

She had her own part to play though because she had to cut off certain friendships, stop watching a number of sexually perverse television programs, definitely cut out all forms of pornography and then delete the numbers of those *common* sexual partners of hers, from her phone. I mean, she had **work** to do—as do we, if we must be set free.

You may say, "Oh, Joys, you're just being too harsh!"—but, we must be strict with ourselves!

It starts out as you watching reality television that says someone became famous through sex tapes and then you google "sample sex tapes." Before long, you start testing the boundaries—exposing your body and from the attention you get, you receive the needed motivation to do it even more. Soon after, some *Lagos big boy* who seems to have some money (which many of them rarely do), will come to ask that you enter a relationship with him. You don't bother to ask God about it because "well, I know He will say 'No' but this is a once in a lifetime opportunity" so you go ahead. You have no idea that he really is a *pimp* so then you go from sleeping with one man to five to ten to fifteen, then you start receiving expensive gifts in exchange. You travel on your favorite airlines (which you've dreamt about for years) first class and then you sleep with more men for more things. Then, you're addicted to sex. Then, "Church? What is that?" Not knowing that you have *made yourself* a **slave** to the world.

In truth, all that this world can never take away from

us is Jesus. Everything else can be ruined in less than one minute. ONLY Christ—the solid rock (not merely the best but the ONLY solid rock)—will stand. So, let's put our focus on and trust in Him.

Are you the girl I just described who has lost her way? Well, run to God right now. Put this book down because it'd still be here when you get back. Go on your knees with your head bowed to the ground and ask God to come into your heart. Ask Him for forgiveness and for His grace and mercy to make you white as snow. Then, ask Him to put His Spirit within you, that will cause you to walk in His ways, keep His statues and do them (Ezekiel 36:27).

I myself prayed this prayer numerous times throughout the latter part of 2015 and one morning as I did my devotion, the Lord was ministering to my heart. He said "ask me to cleanse you of all unrighteousness; and for the grace to keep my commandments, no matter how *terrible*." Oh, what a naturally terrifying prayer. But what joy it brings to one's soul. It is so liberating knowing that all you are and will ever be is in the hands of the all-knowing, all-powerful God.

Just rejoice in Him for one minute and thank Him because your life is in His hands!

all that this world
can never take
away from us is
Jesus.

―――――

It is so liberating
knowing that
all you are and
will ever be is in
the hands of the
all-knowing, all-
powerful God.

What a privilege!

So, decide today: to stop watching those *ratchet* and spiritually deflating television programs, to be faithful in your quality time with Him, to be honest in your dealings and to strive to make God proud, daily.

He sees your heart and if you said that truthfully and wholeheartedly, know that He will help you keep to His Word by keeping to your words. He will activate His Spirit now within you and you so effortlessly will walk in His ways.

That, is the beginning of your greatness.

5

Preserving Our Dignity In Christ

When we think on whom a virgin is today, all we think of is a person who has not had sexual intercourse with another. Some of us single women go about bragging saying, "Oh, I've never had sex with a man—I'm saving myself for my husband. It's so and so that isn't a virgin." Well, congratulations—you're saving yourself for your husband and that's beautiful **BUT** are you also a *virgin* to idolatry?

From Matthew 25 which we earlier examined, the *virgins* were the ones who stayed anxiously awaiting the arrival of the Bridegroom, Jesus. Now, I do not believe that the Bible uses irrelevant words. I believe with all my heart that **all** of God's Word is true and there is no fault in either His letterings or His power.

So, if His Word is true and God really did mean that only the virgins would gloriously await His return, then, what exactly did He mean? More importantly, **how can we be one of those kinds of *virgins*?**

To be a *virgin*, I have found, means to be **free from all sin and blemish, pure and holy in God's sight.** It means to be free from **all** forms of idolatry.

You may read this and say, "well, thank God. I'm not serving any idols!" but, are you sure about that?

You've not made money, fame, *celebrities* or even *that* relationship, your *idol*?

Are you sure?!

Unfortunately, today we live in a world where if you don't have any things or persons as your *idols*, you are considered *weird*. You are expected to literally *live* to become that celebrity or that other celebrity's celebrity—so, we hear story after story about women (and even some men!) getting full-body plastic surgeries to look like a *celebrity*. We watch these *celebrities* on television and think that their lives are all the way perfect so we think to ourselves, "if only I were her."

What a waste of a life if we never let the world enjoy the *quirkiness*, love, person and total awesomeness of **YOU!**

You don't have to be beautiful like her because you were created to be beautiful like YOU!

You don't have to be beautiful like her because you were created to be beautiful like **YOU**! You were made by God to be unique. You were made special. This is why no matter how much you may look like another person, you will have different fingerprints. There is a reason for that—and that is so you know your uniqueness, show your uniqueness and bring others to the likeness of God as you do.

For a season during my teenage years, I sometimes struggled with not feeling *equal* with my siblings. By equal, I mean as special or unique.

I am the fourth and last biological child of my parents and I have super awesome and close-in-age siblings (if you would only meet them, you would love them as much as I do. They're totally the best)! Being five years younger than my immediate older sibling however, only my siblings were pretty much in the same everything growing up—from school to class group—and even had the same circle of friends. Now, *little ol' me* was always the one who had to be friends with the younger siblings of my own siblings' friends because I never liked to go out much. So, if their friends came over, they could bring their own younger siblings and I could have instant playmates. Oh, just imagine the *trauma* that my little heart felt at times when their friends didn't have younger siblings. Lord God—it felt like the *end of the world.* I tried to act grown up so I could at least *fit in* more with my siblings; not realizing that we all were different for a reason and that was what we loved most about each other!

I remember one time when our family travelled to a certain state for a few days. It was my first time there and we got to have a few days off to be family and nothing else. We were in this beautiful one-floor house and there was no hiding place—we were together, ALL of the time. I had been feeling so misunderstood and my teenage self was used to running high off of emotions that I suddenly started crying. For those who know me, you know that *THAT,* is so not me.

Anyway, it became even more frustrating when the ENTIRE family gathered together to discuss my *pain.* Oh goodness, now it was the topic of discussion and we needed to discuss our *feelings.* So, I poured out my heart (or so I thought), and I was expecting the same to be reciprocated. Well, when it came time for my brothers, they literally just burst into laughter. It seemed like their laughs even were synchronized. I mean, really, "I pour out my teenage heart to you and all you can do is laugh?!" Still all up in my feelings, I said, **"don't you know I'm just a teenager?"** Oh, better believe that my brothers haven't let that one go. It gets to be the weight of every *Joys joke* every once in a while;

but today, looking back at that is so much fun! I'm not in my feelings as I used to be so laughter is more of my response. I thank God that I have made progress and I'm in my place of strong conviction that nothing or no one can make me believe—ever—that I am not exactly who God made me to be. I am just as special as my sister, brothers, or the next person. I am beautiful, in every way, and God looks to smile at me daily **because** I live to love Him more.

My family was and is always so accepting and we accept each other as we are, and love each other to the perfection of Christ—as He wills. Our family tradition always has been and is LOVE and so, we live to breathe, eat, sleep and *love* Love. Oh, what a blessing it is that Christ Himself is Love.

So, as many times as people who know little or next to nothing about my family try to compare me to my siblings, my response is **love**. I mean, what a blessing it is to have absolutely no competitiveness to the point of belittling, fighting, or undermining one another in a family. If we were all the same, we would be so boring. Our differences are what make us a strong unit and YOUR differences are what also make you special. Absolutely **NO ONE** has what you've got—so don't let the world miss the uniqueness of you!

I have gone through all of this to say that you do not

need to desire someone else's life. You were made special and unique by God for a reason and once you discover and walk in that, "all other things will be added to you (Matthew 6:33)."

Maybe you haven't been strongly convicted yet and your thing is dealing with sexual immorality. You sleep with every man that has a pulse: married men and/or even that one guy you are in a relationship with but that is not your husband. Maybe you've made that relationship your idol. Well, today, **you have got to let it go! If God isn't in it, neither should you.**

You might even be in a godly relationship: with a man who loves God with all his heart, mind, soul, and spirit—but you choose him over God; you must change that too. Whether you are in a courtship or married, yes, you should love your partner (soon-to-be spouse)/spouse as the man God has put in your life to lead you in His ways—but you must **not** put him before God. This may sound somewhat ridiculous; you might be saying, if he loves God then why would I need more restrictions in this relationship?

Thing though is that **anything that you place higher than God, is your idol.**

You may need to re-evaluate your priorities and as much as you love that man (for those in godly relationships), love God 100 times more. Don't stop loving your spouse—absolutely not!—just love God more. Serve Him more. Be more dedicated to Him—and you would see that there is absolutely no way it wouldn't positively impact on your relationship as well.

So, evaluate yourself today.

What is that thing that you have placed above God in your life? What has taken God's place?

Now is the time to make the change—now is the time to put God back on the highest pedestal; it is where He belongs.

Now is the time to
put God back on the
highest pedestal.

6

Does Judgement Day Scare You?

I recently daily read the Book of Revelation, for a season. Through the letters and the chapters, all I could sense was Christ. I felt Him holding my hand as I flipped through the pages, I felt Him hold me by my shoulders and squeeze me in for big hugs a number of times, and I even felt myself laying on His chest, hearing His heartbeat. This is consistently my desire with God and interestingly, I felt it while also reading the Book of REVELATION—the Book that *scares* us Christian folk, the most.

So, if I may, let me ask you this question:

When you read or hear about *judgement* day, rapture, and/or the *end times*, what comes to your heart: fear *or* excitement?

This is a very critical question and I would hope that you will be honest answering it, to yourself. God can *only* work with the truth. He can work with you saying, "Lord, I'm a liar, a cheat, a fornicator, a thief, a molester, an adulterer, a broken man... I ask that You forgive me of my many sins and help me walk in Your ways. Become my Truth and help me grow in You." God can work with that. He will wash you so clean that even you will know that your sins now are far away from you. He will heal your wounds: your brokenness, hurt, pain, worry-full heart, anxiety etc. He wants to do that ALL for you and give you *life*. You may say, "but I already am alive! I am reading this book right now"— but on your best days, you merely exist, if you don't have Christ.

He says in Deuteronomy 30:19, "Today I have given you the choice between life and death... Oh, that you would choose life, so that you and your descendants might live!" Christ is the life that we live. Our spirit is the true life—so without an active spirit, we are merely human-like robots, walking to an unknown destination, but walking. There is no difference between such a person and a *zombie* (a walking but dead being). Any functioning adult living a blessed life would choose life over death and with the blessed opportunity we have to live this life, I pray that you too, will choose life. I pray that you will choose life Himself; I pray that you will choose God. Also remember, your choices do not only affect you; they affect your *descendants*. So do you want a living generation or a zombie generation? The choice is yours, and it all begins with an honest heart.

I hear some people say, "Well, I'm an atheist. I don't believe in anything."

Truth is, without realizing it, you may even have more faith than many *trying* Christians! You believe that there is no God but are well enough to plan out your clothes for the next morning, setting up appointments and all—well assured that you'd wake up the next day breathing and in good health? How? What is it that would keep you through the night, wake you up in the morning, allow your brain to function, and then keep it functioning? Or, you think it all just is supposed to happen? You have faith in each passing moment and therefore have faith in a God, in THE GOD, without even knowing. You have faith and you didn't even know it! You're believing in something, in *Someone*, but are just not deciding to say it aloud.

I once had someone tell me that she believed in a higher power but just not that it could be God.

In truth, I pray that she comes to know the God that I know. The loving, sweet, Heavenly Father that I serve.

God knows our heart but needs our *admission* to set us free.

Remember the scripture we read earlier in this chapter? God said, "... *CHOOSE* life..." It's all a matter of choice. God will never force Himself on anyone. He was so amazing to give to us a *will* (that is, the ability to make our own choices), when He created us. That's true love at work. Could He have made us all robots, running around doing only what He *tuned* us to do for the day? Absolutely! Did He? No. I tell you, there is absolutely no stronger love and trust than that. He trusted, hoped, and had faith enough in us to make the right choice. So, I pray today that we do make that *right* choice.

If you are a Christian, fully surrendered to God, but you still have that fear when it comes to judgment day, you need to run to the feet of the Father. Fear does not come from God. It comes from the devil *alone* and so for you to have it, you *took* it. It is time to **give it back** to that devil. **You have the mind and heart of Christ; so why take on the emotions of the devil?**

Listen, trust me when I say I *hate* fear. I've contended with it, many times.

There were seasons when all I wanted to do was run home to my parents and crawl up on their bed because

God knows our heart but needs our admission to set us free.

I felt almost crippled by fear but instead, I took up my bottle of oil, anointed my home and myself, sprinkled the blood of Jesus, said a quick prayer, and went to bed—comfortably. Why? Because I trust in God *more than* I trust in fear. Fear may be real, but my God is more real to me. Now, does that mean the devil wouldn't want to test me with fears? Absolutely not! But my confidence is in a God who says that though the devil comes one way, he WILL flee 7 ways! My God is so much stronger and He's got my back—this, I am sure of!

Now, you may be battling with your own fear or even surrounded by many fears—the fears of "will I ever get married?," "will my husband ever love me like so and so's husband?," "is my life over?," "am I ever going to be successful?," or, the more popular "when will my own time come?" You may be bothered with these fears or even the simple ones of lizards falling off the wall into your bed, a cockroach *staring at you* when you merely woke up to use the bathroom at night, or the in the moment fears such as, "will this plane crash?!"

All in all, these fall in the same bracket; they are all *fears*. Now, I Peter 5: 11 (The Voice) says,

"For all power belongs to God, now and forever."

So, God is greater than the power of fear. He is greater than the bondage that fear could ever have on you—and

He is greater, for you. So, whenever those thoughts of fear come in, you must *cast* them down (II Corinthians 10:5). You are greater than your fears because God is greater than they, and He lives within you (Galatians 2:20)! He doesn't live beside you, having to physically pull you saying, "Come on, let's run from this fear," No! He lives on your inside and when you let Him flow through you, those fears are immediately cast down.

How, you may ask?

Remember we talked about growing in our relationship with God earlier? Well, you need to grow in Him daily and the more you do, the more you give Him control in and over your life. When you do that, He becomes more alive in you. It all is a matter of choice and consistency in that choice.

Lastly, if you are a born again Christian and have total excitement when you read or hear about the *rapture*, I rejoice with you! Your heart is with the Father and I pray it never goes anywhere else.

7

Coloured Friendships

One morning right before I began my Bible study, it was impressed on my heart so strongly to pray for my friends. What was to be a few words of prayer turned into a long while of thanksgiving and prayer. I prayed for them one after the other and was specific in my asking of the Lord, as I knew each one's situations and desires. For direction, discretion, focus, success, leading, and my favourite of all, a heart closer to the Father. Interestingly though, these friends that I poured my heart out to God for, were only four in number.

Isn't it interesting? Only four friends, you may ask; really? Well, yes. Let me ask you this. Have you ever tried praying for your friends? For no just reason but just, well, because? Have you sat down to appreciate

God for the friendships that you do have or taken a day out for sole appreciation to God because of those friendships and nothing else? Have you taken a day out specifically to fast and pray for your friends? Because if you have, you would realize for yourself that your circle of friends truly is so small. How many people are you willing to pray and thank God for—for an entire day? How many are you willing to fast for? How many are you truly grateful to God for, knowing that no matter what happens, those days, months, or years of friendship were a blessing to you? Friendships are important and real friends are very rare; so, when you find true, God-focused friendships, keep them. When the relationships are devil-entertaining, do not at all entertain them; but pray for the hearts of the individuals themselves (whether they be male or female), to be turned to the Lord. Yes, those friendships may not be yours to claim anymore but the people who you had those friendships with, still are loved by your Heavenly Father. So, pray for them—pray that they return to the bosom of Christ.

Question then is, **how do you know your real friends?**

Let's begin with the last statement I made regarding true friendships. I said that they are God-focused.

Like anyone else, I've had interestingly different friendships. I've had the wonderfully seasoned friendships, the worry-filled seasoned friendships, the "I-love-God-but-I-just-don't-act-like-it" friendships, the "lets-love-God-together-but-still-maybe-be-physically-intimate" friendships and the friendships that purely point you towards Christ.

Let me say this right now.

ANY *friend* who does not push you closer to God is not God-ordained, for you.

Now, I don't mean the ones who solely *tell* you to love God more with words or encourage you to do so while they do the exact opposite but ones who talk, act, and live Christ.

Do you know what that means? That means at times when they least feel like doing so, they love Christ the most. In moments when you would expect them to give you mentally soothing but God-defying advice, they seek to push you towards God. I mean, have you ever been pushed to your *limit* and then you did something you knew was totally wrong but felt that when you told your friend, they'd at least be on your side? And then you tell them and… **they're not**. They tell you that you could have handled it differently and ask you two to pray together so that God grants you even greater wisdom for the next time a similar situation reoccurs. Have you ever just wanted to revel in your wrongs and then your friend asks that you both pray, so you wouldn't repeat the same mistakes? Believe me, I know—it can be momentarily, least satisfying.

My mother and sister are two of my absolute best friends and with the amount of time I spend with my mother—working together, practically living together, often travelling together—there's no doubt she knows most of what happens in my life (particularly because I love to involve her in it all). Now, she has a whole lot of wisdom and her love for me is unquestionable; so those things never are the issue. But there are times: I may be in the wrong in a situation (and am honest enough to admit it to myself); but while telling her, in that very moment, I solely want to vent and not necessarily pray for even more wisdom. Those moments, I want to revel in my wrongs—but thank God for faithful, strong, and beautiful women like her in my life; who can tell me with all love and care that I was wrong but God has the power to make all wrongs right, if I let Him.

Around the time I began writing this chapter, a good friend of mine asked if she could talk to me on some issues. We talk quite often (that is, every couple of days, at the least), and so when she sends me messages like that, I know that it somewhat relates to *boy* troubles. She mentioned to me how she was not at all attracted to this one guy who took actions that made her believe he was attracted to her—but instead of addressing it and possibly clearing things up with him so that there was an understanding of where she stood with him, she made an interesting statement. She said to me, "I just want to keep my options open." I paused. Way back in my past, I would have just let that *slide*. We would laugh over it, maybe joke about it for a couple more conversations, but would eventually let it go. This time though, it struck an interesting cord with me because of the relationship that I, now, had built with my Father.

I said to her, "Sweets, doing that is not at all fair; either to him or to you. He may be too shy to speak up but you aren't. You can address it so that you both know where you stand and in that, there would be no confusion. Also, if you *string* him along, you would have to give account to God for that because you really have no valid reason to." I said, "Then again, God knows you, loves you and has all these amazing plans for you. What if the man God has ready for you then avoids making his approach because he thinks you're in a relationship with this other man? All in all, you have to be cautious about making God proud and I doubt He would be, right now, regarding this."

It seemed she only part-listened to all I said and she said she would try to speak with this guy, days later, to clear it up. She made it clear to me that she wasn't making any promises and wouldn't guarantee that she would do it. About two days later, we spoke again and I asked her if she eventually decided to say something to him. She said to me, "I spoke to him that same night and cleared it up." It caught me a bit off guard but made me so proud of her. She wanted a *friend* to help her revel in her wrongs but she didn't find one in me. The kind she found in me was the God-kind; the kind that lovingly opens your eyes to your wrongs and loves you more towards Jesus.

If you don't have friends like these, you need to ask the Holy Spirit to bring them your way; and when He does, make sure to keep them growing.

It is important to know that every friendship is a living entity; and just like any living thing, it must be fed to survive. So I have to ask you, do you feed your friendships? Do you try to keep tabs on your friends and see how they're doing or if they need some of your assistance? Do you pray for them and commit them to the hands of the Father? **What do you do to feed your friendships**; because if you feed it with nothing, it WILL die.

It is also important to note that it is not only feeding these friendships that matters but also what they are being fed with. If you have a plant and instead of *feeding* it with water daily, you decide to *feed* it *Coldstone* ice-cream, it would have a few growth issues, to say the least. If you decide it should eat rice, it would have even more problems because all it needs is simply, water.

Every friendship is
a living entity.

Growing In Faith

Water may seem over-simplistic but really, that is all it needs. So, what you feed your friendships with is greatly important. Feed it with the Word of God, with prayers, with love and with care. If I asked you right now: Of the last 50 messages you sent to your friends, was there any one that focused on building their *spirit man*? When was the last time you invested in prayers for your friends or loved them out of their pain? When last did you care for them like you care for yourself (Mark 12:31)? All of these are important, because feeding your godly friendships, cannot be overemphasized.

Then, how often you feed these friendships also is important. As I mentioned earlier, most plants require daily amounts of water for proper growth just as most friendships require daily amounts of the Word, prayers, love, and care to survive. You don't have to speak over the phone or see each other daily but, how often do you take these friends up in prayers and how readily available are you when they need you? If your friend had one call in a time of trouble, could they count on you? Your love and care, proven through your actions, aid the growth of your friendships; and lack thereof, would lead to *death* and destruction.

8
Your Friends Know Who You Are

Recently, when a friend of mine was going through some trouble. His sister was sick and he needed someone to pray with/for her. He was extremely desperate, and wanted someone he could trust; someone whose prayers, he could trust. Many would assume that for the most part, I get messages that ask for my father to pray for others, when they are sick or in need of other prayers—and this is true; but for the most part, not from my friends. This is because they know my stance in/with God, and in what areas they have seen Him answer my prayers, speedily.

So, this friend of mine sent me a message briefly narrating what had happened with his sister and asking that I say a word of prayer. He said to me, "I know God answers you in this area." You know, that struck me, although not in that moment; because I was too focused on *ensuring* the healing. God gave us the Christian/ Christ- followership mandate when He said,

"15And then he told them, 'Go into all the world and preach the [Gospel] to everyone. 16 Anyone who believes and is baptized will be saved. But anyone who refuses to believe will be condemned. 17 These miraculous signs will accompany those who believe: They will cast out demons in my name, and they will speak in new languages. 18 They will be able to handle snakes with safety, and if they drink anything poisonous, it won't hurt them. **They will be able to place their hands on the sick, and they will be healed**.'" Mark 16: 15- 18 (NLT).

I had just begun increasingly walking in the reality of this Scripture when that message came in. For reasons known only to God, He let me read that message only a few hours later (and my friends know that that in itself is a miracle), and then, I sent out a word of prayer. I told him to remain at peace, after I sent him the two-lined prayer, and I said to him to let me know when the victory was visible—that same day.

It was interesting because I did not hear from him until the next day and his message had a sigh of relief *written* all over it. The air no longer seemed stuffy and I knew the victory had come, once I opened the message to read this reply. He apologized for not getting back in touch with me the day prior. He said that she had gone from almost being in a coma to now, being completely healed. She was strengthened, could talk, and also, could eat (and now you know when a sick patient can eat, THAT is victory)!

It was a blessing to hear that testimony, and thereafter was when I began thinking on that statement he had earlier made.

Truth is, your friends know who you are.

They know if you're the friend they can ask to pray and if you're not. They know if you can be trusted with their deepest, darkest secrets, possibly from a time when they hadn't surrendered fully to the Lord, and they know if you're the Judas of the group. Your friends know who you are. They may act as though they do not care, not even knowing that they do this; but on that day when they need a true friend, they know whether or not to call you.

Are you a friend, or are you a foe in friend-ly clothing?

Have your friends ever called for your opinion and listened to the same, or do they have to call eight other people to be sure that you are steering them in the right

Your friends know
who you are.

way? Thing is, there are black and white friendships, and there are coloured friendships. Some friendships bring doom while others, bring colour.

In the parable of the Prodigal son accounted in Luke 15, we see that the prodigal son asked his father for his portion of his inheritance because he wanted to leave home. Maybe he had friends who encouraged him daily to do that, or others who encouraged him to do so with their Instagram-worthy pictures all over their Before Christ (BC) social media life. Maybe he just had consistent fantasies of what it would be like to live in control of his own money, or a combination of them all.

You know, I recently saw an episode of this television show about young adults who were born in wealth and sadly, know how to use up all that invested money of their parents, all too *well*. I saw these two teenagers who went into a Rolls Royce dealership and one child encouraged the other to buy one of these cars as his first car; of course, with his father's credit card. This other boy didn't want to, but this friend was pushing him so hard, he finally said okay. Thankfully, the car was sold out already and so he got some more time, though unwanted, to think on this decision before making such a *wasteful* purchase—that is, at his age, with money he really knew that he couldn't spend. Thing is, based off of our friendships, we can very easily be pushed. Pushed to do things that maybe on a normal day, we would not do. You know, you may hate pornography, with all of your spirit, soul, and body—but then you have *this* friend. Oh no, they would never force you. Maybe they entice you with the garbage television shows that are almost entirely filled with nudity. Then you watch the movies with similar characteristics. Then, you watch them continuously. Then, you never go a day without watching them. Then, while checking for those movies online, you see a link to a pornography site that says something like, "Just check her out. It really isn't that bad." You don't know what to do, so you leave the page open; and the devil keeps telling you that one nude picture isn't that bad, and everybody watches porn even if they do not say so. Then, you click to that site—and then before you know it, it's a monthly, weekly, daily, unavoidable habit.

All of it because you wanted to *please* a friend who wasn't God-ordained for you, in the first place.

There is such an anointing that friends have on us.

In verse 24 of Luke 15 mentioned above, the Bible says:

"For this my son was dead, and is alive again; he was lost, and is found..." (KJV)

The father called his son dead—all because he departed

from the home in which he was protected.

Maybe you have left the fold in which you know that the protective hand of God is strong on your life. Maybe you are hanging around the type of friends that the prodigal son had, who encouraged him to leave the home—the friends who encourage you to go watch nude movies, to go support the gay parades (because *it is the Christian thing to do to support love* and *all love is real love?*).

Do not be deceived.

God has beautiful, godly friendships in view for you, and all that you have to do is prepare yourself for them by being that godly friend yourself.

Be that godly friend, and you will be surprised that even if you are lost or feel lost, you will be found, and made alive, again.

There's this friend of mine who I've experienced a number of life seasons with. In nine years of friendship, I can honestly say that we have learnt a lot from each other, taught a lot to each other, and pray ceaselessly for one another. I remember talking with him one day and after joking about something for a little while, he said, "I'll pray for you about that." I'm pretty sure that he had said that countless times before; but this day, it meant something more. He always has been the *behind-the-*

scenes prayer *warrior*. He prays ceaselessly for those he loves, and expects almost nothing in return. He is selfless in himself, and that is one quality that I have always greatly admired.

You know, in reading through the Bible Book of Daniel, I discovered even more about coloured friendships.

Do you know that Daniel, Shadrach, Meshach, and Abednego were friends before they were brought in as captives? And then, they remained friends until after their training, even when they entered the royal service—THREE YEARS LATER (See Daniel 1:5, 18-19)!

There is a place for seasonal friendships, as God deems fit; oh, but the beauty of long-term friendships, one will never be able to fully explain.

I have been blessed with friendships ranging from seven to over ten years so I have experienced some of the beauty that they bring—and Daniel and his three friends show us beauty in the same.

My prayer is that God blesses you with such healthy long-term friendships, where your purpose will be to serve God irrespective of the *consequences* from/by the world.

Reading this, at this point, you might think that by now, you know all four of my friends. Thankfully

The beauty of long-term friendships, one will never be able to fully explain.

though, from the time I began writing this chapter until now, God has blessed me with even more beautiful friendships. "Now more than four?" you might ask, and to that, I say, YES!

God knows how to bring that colour to your life—and really, all you need to do is start by BEING that good friend.

9
The Sickle Of Competition

> *"¹⁴ But if you are bitterly jealous and there is selfish ambition in your heart, don't cover up the truth with boasting and lying. ¹⁵ For jealousy and selfishness are not God's kind of wisdom. Such things are earthly, unspiritual, and demonic."*
>
> James 3: 14-15 (NLT)

In today's world, there is so much bitterness, jealously, and envy. Even great friendships have been torn apart on entry of these qualities. They come into your heart, sink deep down into the same, and weary you until you are torn apart; all of you, including your godly friendships. You know, there are times that the devil tries all he can and gives it his best shot but still gets no victory in your life; well, unfortunately, not until he utilizes the tool of social media.

In my life, I have found that social media is one of the devil's greatest tools to destroying great friendships.

You start your day off beautifully, log on to Instagram and after 45 minutes of examining everyone else's pages, you come to the realization that you are not like anyone else. Thing is, instead of seeing this as a positive, you see it as such a negative, and you begin to hurt yourself emotionally, because **God made you so different**!

Suddenly, social media has made you think that being the same as everyone else is more beauty that the true beauty of your very own uniqueness.

Galatians 5: 24- 26 says,

> "**[24] Those who belong to Christ Jesus have nailed the passions and desires of their sinful nature to his cross and crucified them there.** [25] *Since we are living by the Spirit, let us follow the Spirit's leading in every part of our lives.* [26] **Let us not** *become conceited, or provoke one another, or* **be jealous of one another."** *(NLT)*

It is important that I state here and now that social media in itself is not the devil. The thoughts that the devil puts in our minds that we are not enough, utilizing the channel of social media as we let him, is where the problem is—and we must face it, head on.

You know, I have a few personal social media accounts.

The Sickle Of Competition

I remember when I had only a hundred or so friends on Facebook and it was a place to go for a laugh. My friends and I would log on at about the same time, look out for things we loved, and share those loud laughs (at one another), with one another. We would tag each other at the bottom of the funniest (or so we thought) pictures, and we would have as much fun as we could, for the few minutes we got to share together.

Today though, things are very different.

With an increasing social media followership, it has turned from a place of laughs with friends to a place of public opinion. In life, I see everything God gives as a blessing—including the opportunity to be a blessing through the channel of social media—but one thing that this growth has taught me is that, there is no need to rush through any phase. Each phase is a building phase and unless we live a life that is pleasing to God, everything that social media brings will only be but fleeting, in-the-moment pleasure.

You know, I had this friend—who I seemed to have a stable relationship with, but eventually, turned out to be a relationship not built on *good* ground (Matthew 7:24-27). The wind of social media comparisons blew, and that relationship went tumbling down!

I love how the Bible puts it when He says,

There is no need to rush through any phase.

The Sickle Of Competition

> *"... it is foolish, like a person who builds a house on sand.* **27 When the rains and floods come and the winds beat against that house,** *it will collapse with a mighty crash.'"*
>
> *Matthew 7:26-27 (NLT)*

We had talked several times about several things, but then God began to take me through this phase of accelerated growth, on social media. Maybe it just was my turn and two days later would have been her turn, who knows! —but she was not ready to be second to see the growth. She didn't realize that it never takes time, it only takes God.

During one of our conversations, I mentioned something about a recent post I had made on social media and the seeming backlash it brought. I explained how being so blessed with a new sea of opinions taught me to stand stronger in my faith, and in God. Others began making their comments and I listened intently (because with friends, you never know when your Word from God, through them, would come). In only but a little while, this *friend* spoke up and said, "oh, is it because you now have more followers than me?" this was the beginning of the friendship breakdown because in *real* friendships, it is **never** about who has more *followers* than the other.

This was someone I well respected and so, it came

to me as a shock. The expressions—and actions—that followed these words made it more apparent that it was not a joke. I tried to resolve it by having a conversation with this friend about the same, but it didn't turn out too well. It had been in her heart for a while and finally, out of the abundance of what was within, the words emanated from her mouth (Matthew 12:34). Her mind was made up and our friendship was nothing more than a competition of who could have more *followers* which was to me, just not worth it.

Friendships built on competition will never last.

You know, we talk about healthy competition, but if everyone is running their own race, no one else is on your track.

Yes, it is good to have friends who positively impact on your walk with God just as Daniel, Shadrach, Meshach, and Abednego did for one another; but we must be careful not to make it into competition. The more important things in life cannot be rightly assessed using the rubric of another.

You may compete about who can read the Bible cover to cover the fastest but can you accurately measure who God speaks to more through His Word? You may compete about who hears the voice of God more but can you ascertain that it is His voice, every single time?

The Sickle Of Competition

You may compete about the darkness of your skin or the paleness of your eyes but can you truly discover who has the covenant of long life most activated in them?

There are many people to compare yourself to and so many things to compare yourselves in; there always will be—but until you make your purpose the pursuit of God and nothing else, competition will eat you up.

"A peaceful heart leads to a healthy body; jealousy is like cancer in the bones." Proverbs 14: 30 (NLT)

I heard the story of how Oral Roberts, T. L. Osborn, and Kenneth E. Hagin lived together at a point in their lives. They were life-long friends, lived in the same city, had vibrant and notable ministries, but **never** struggled with the spirit of competition.

Yes, it is a spirit—a tactic of the devil to keep you from walking your walk and making **your impact.** It is his tactic—but my prayer today is that you will be strong enough to resist its holds, in Jesus name.

> Love, endlessly.
>
> Pray, ceaselessly.
>
> Favour, completely.

In this, you would know whether you truly have friends or just distant acquaintances for the sake of seemingly avoiding loneliness.

Until you make your purpose the pursuit of God and nothing else, competition will eat you up.

"**The followers argued among themselves about which of them would be the greatest**. ⁴⁷ Jesus knew what they were thinking. He put a child beside Him. ⁴⁸ He said to the followers, 'Whoever receives this child in My name, receives Me. Whoever receives Me, receives Him Who sent Me. **The one who is least among you is the one who is great.**'" Luke 9:46-48 (NLV)

10
What Your Eyes See And Ears Hear

The day I began writing this chapter, I had been greatly overwhelmed. The *Women Of The God Kind* website was about to launch and one thing most people did not know was, I designed it all myself. I dug deep into *css* (which I previously knew nothing about); and with countless calls and online chats with my hosting company plus a sample template (thank Jesus for *Wordpress*!), I had my start. I designed it all in 4 days but the more I did, the more I felt I needed to do. This time though, there was no going back! Having announced it on social media days prior, now it HAD to happen.

This, alongside my full time jobs (as I was in a new

position at work but still had to cover my old position until someone else officially take over), my doctoral coursework (as I now had been working at my degree for a little over a year with absolutely no breaks but the two weeks I got at Christmas), writing articles for my column on my mother's website (*www.faithoyedepo.org*), helping my sister out with her new beautiful baby girl, and then travels, I felt overwhelmed. Sometimes, it even felt like I was running on fumes; but I was determined.

I had this new found love for God and all things His Word so I decided I would fill myself up with more of Him, as much as I could, daily. First things first, I would give no place to my *feelings* of not wanting to read my Bible on any given day.

Yes, I have those *feelings* too.

There are times when I would rather curl up in my bed and snooze but I recently began to tell myself, I WILL study the Word of God instead. I remember one of such mornings, not too long after I had made this commitment, I was listening to an old-time Billy Graham message. He was talking about how studying our Bible and praying daily would eventually lead us to the place where we would get up in the mornings and have a "*spring* in our step." I caught that word so strongly and was eager to have that be my daily experience. So, on this particular day—the day I began

What Your Eyes See And Ears Hear

writing this Chapter—I had that *very* experience. I had just read my Bible in the morning (a new version that I had just purchased), & on praying and worshipping God right after the study, all I could feel, was *pure* joy! This, was Heaven's joy. It felt so real and so beautiful that I remember saying in that moment, "Lord, thank you that I can feel that *spring* in my step!" I tell you—the joy of the Lord is so real.

Can you imagine if I decided not to spend the first hours of my day that morning with the Lord? I might have ended up being upset with everyone or carrying such a *long*, unhappy face throughout my day.

Yes, there will be distractions. There will be reasons for you to go somewhere or read something or do something else. There would be seemingly valid reasons why you *can't* spend your morning with the Lord. We must remember though that He comes FIRST.

I remember an experience I had a couple months ago which I am not at all proud of. I was at work, going about my duties with a staff of my office. We were scouting some locations for interviews we were set to hold the next day. The day was filled with so many stress-worthy events and I was in a hurry not to let any second go wasted. Plus, it was Wednesday (meaning, church service at 6pm—well known to every Winners Chapel International church member). Amid it all, a certain guy who had caused a lot of troubles for myself and most of

The joy of the Lord is
so real.

my friends and/or colleagues, showed up. This time, he was not backing down with his antics and was ready to cause at the very least, some drama, it seemed. I tried to walk away but was followed. The bickering back and forth led me to standing right in front of his face, addressing him, and then walking away, quite angrily. I raised my voice to the point that some other workers in my office complex came out to see what was happening. Mind you, this all happened with that certain staff from my office, there. Was I embarrassed? Absolutely! Did it need to get to that point? Absolutely not. Could I have handled it much better? Definitely! But… I did not read my Bible that morning. I did not spend time with my Saviour on that day.

Yes, I was busy. Yes, I had a lot of pressing issues continuously come up. Yes, it seemed like too much all at once; but the time with God was most important on that day, and is most important today.

If we don't spend time with the Creator, how can we understand His creation? Many of us say, "Oh, I have three kids and I'm a single mom and I have to cook, clean, wash dishes and then make the money. There's no way I can spend time with God." But Miss, you have the time to watch television. You have the time to call your friends and gossip (yes, gossip), about that sister who doesn't dress upscale enough or doesn't know how to match colours or has the *ugly* kids. Miss, you have the time for those other forfeitable things; so, how then don't you have the time to spend with God?

I tell you the truth in Christ and I lie not: 21 unbroken days of true fellowship with the Almighty God will change your life.

We have the time for whatever we have the time for.

Have you ever tried to calculate how much time you spend on social media? How many hours you spend daily on *Facebook, twitter, Instagram, periscope, google+* and the likes, every day? Have you tried to go a day without your phone? These things seem so petty but we must *Count the cost,* as the Bible says.

If I were to ask you right now,

Do you love your phone more than you love God? Yes/ No.

Do you love your friends more than you love God? Yes/ No.

Do you love your family more than you love God? Yes/ No.

Would you sacrifice your life for the God Who sacrificed His life for you? Yes/ No.

Most of us would answer in the affirmative that we love God.

If this is true though, why are we not as addicted to God as we are to our phones? For some of us if a thief comes in to steal your Bible, you may not realise

We have the time for whatever we have the time for.

it for months, if ever; but if a thief stole your phone?! At 2am you'd be waking all your neighbours, searching houses—until that phone was found!

So, where's your love? Where's your heart and your true devotion?

We need to reorder our priorities. We cannot keep asking God to give us His best but then we're giving Him... nothing.

I know this because I've been there. I too, had to train my heart and soul to long for the Saviour. I had to set boundaries and put my phone down until my Bible was first picked up. I had to stop listening to trash music, including those that we love to say "oh, they're just love songs", and settle on God-songs. I had to stop watching trash television expecting to be cleansed. Is this extreme? Absolutely not! I still have a long way to go to complete and total **mind purity**.

You may have picked up this book, now contemplating putting it down for 40 minutes, just so you can catch up on the newest *Real Housewives* episode—and then you'd be back. Maybe you just even came from watching one of such episodes or are doing so on your laptop as we speak. With all those pictures of fornication, inappropriate dressing, cussing, lying and cheating, how can you expect to hear the voice of the Lord? Our minds get so cluttered with earthly things that no matter how loudly God screams, we may never hear.

Imagine being in the ocean and seeing someone about to get bitten by a shark. You try to scream, all under water, but he doesn't hear you. You tried—you screamed as loud as you could, but the sound vibrations did the other man no good. Though it was the other person who may have found himself in the wrong situation, you feel guilty because you tried and really did want to help but it just wasn't *enough*. The sound vibrations just weren't enough.

It's the same thing with God and you—and your ocean sound-clouding reality television messes!

Believe me when I say that I was there too. I loved to catch up on these shows until one day God showed me that what television does is "tell-you-a-vision."

Dictionary.com defines

Vision [vizh-uh n]: the act or power of anticipating that which will or may come to be:

So, it means that unless you are watching something that you would love to see become your own future, it may be time to turn it off. Your life is way too precious to give it all away for a 40 minute television mess. As I say often: YOU are too precious in God's sight and the world needs your light (Matthew 5:14). The distractions will never stop—but with Christ, you are so much stronger than they. So, say <u>NO</u> to the distractions and **YES** to Jesus—again and again and again; every single day.

*what television does is
"tell-you-a-vision."*

11

Through The Noise

One question I have been asked time without number is, "Can God speak through the noise?" That is, "even when I act stubborn and don't feel like listening, can God still speak to me through other ways to be sure that I hear Him—but not to the point that I'm hurt?"

People say, well, God still spoke to Jonah. He still accepted the people of Israel after their whining and complaining. He listened to *this* person and *that* person and gave *that* other person good results, still!

Well, would you rather be a crumb falling from the table or the *main* course?

In Matthew 17 and from verse 22, Jesus speaking to

a Canaanite woman who worshipped and asked for His help said,

"It is not appropriate to take the children's bread and throw it to the dogs!" (WEB)

He eventually gave the woman her heart's desire but what did He mean when He said He wouldn't cast the bread meant for the children to the *dogs*? Who exactly are the *dogs*?! Did He mean a literal dog or was it in reference to a person or thing?

Well, if we read through to verse 28, we see that He meant the children not of Him. Now, Jesus was in no way degrading women; He just would rather run after those running after Him than those running from Him yet expecting Him to work for them.

Yes, He came for the LOST. He runs to save the lost and craves that their hearts be turned toward Him but God isn't merely your chequebook, *gimme gimme* imaginary Being, or servant. He is Christ. He is Lord. **He is Saviour of ALL.**

It's time to stop the deceit and run into His arms just as much as He is pulling you to Himself. Imagine this: you are running toward God as He also runs towards you, to grab you, hold you to Himself and twirl you around; not letting go. How beautiful! —the King of ALL kings running toward you! Why wouldn't you want to experience this?

Back to the question above though, just as God spoke to Jonah, yes, He absolutely can speak to you through the noise but why desire that when you can have such a joyful, peaceful and restful relationship with Him— hugging and **hearing His heart beat all of the time**. Personally, the moments when I do *feel* this way are my absolute favourite.

A lady recently shared with me, her story. She said she was deep into fornication and loved the *excitement* that came with sleeping around with men; at any time. She did however, always feel convicted right after. She would run from God and please her flesh but then she would run to her Bible and ask God why He wasn't there, the nights when she had no man in her bed but wanted to feel *hugged on*.

> **NOTE:** *Now is the time to interject and say to you:* **You can never serve this world and expect to enjoy the benefits of one who serves the Word.**

Matthew 6: 24 (NIV) says,

> *"No one can serve two masters, for either he will hate the one and love the other; or else he will be devoted to one and despise the other..."*

Do not believe the world when they say you can

proclaim Christ yet rap with lyrics that cuss at everything that breathes. Don't settle with the notion that you can serve Christ yet be *devoted* to fornication. You can ONLY have and serve ONE master. **YOU make the choice**.

This lady told me that God would convict her through dreams, the words of people close to her and even during those *strange* Bible studies and late night prayer times. He convicted her through as many means and as many times as seemed possible—but she would resist and still have men in her bed at night. Little by little though, the seed was being planted. Her desire to please God slowly but steadily began to grow. Instead of having a man in her bed every night, she would have them in her bed 3 nights a week, and then 2 nights a week **and then not at all.** It wasn't right even when she had men in her bed 2 nights a week but she didn't give up. God didn't give up! His love and consistency **stole** away her *fleshy* desires and now all she wants is to please God with all of her being.

How awesome is God?! **He pushes through the noise** and ensures that those who run away from Him the most are given opportunity after opportunity to surrender themselves to Him.

Imagine if someone had God convicting them through

You can ONLY have and serve ONE master.

His Holy Spirit daily for months and they kept running. Then, they *pass away* because of whatever situation/circumstance. On judgement day, they would not have the excuse that they never heard the Word of God or that they weren't given the opportunity to surrender themselves to Him.

It might sound awesome to have God running after you in a game of *tit-for-tat* but the risk of hell is far too great. You do not want to be sent to the "burning lake of sulphur" (NLT) and so, the other option of total peace, serenity, joy, love and prosperity in Jesus is so much sweeter.

It's time that you followed hard after God.

If you are missing your way, He WILL speak to you through the noise but do **NOT** let that be His only avenue of loving on you and talking with you. **Truly be His bride and *Skype* with Him daily with open arms and an open heart.**

12

The Lesser Job

On one beautiful Sunday, I had the opportunity to take a quick trip with my parents for the afternoon. I absolutely love such trips because when my parents get together with their friends and/or mentors, I just get to listen in on their conversations and I leave almost always feeling like I have a much more renewed mind in Christ; they all just speak with so much wisdom. On our way back, I was thinking on how God always does what He says He will do but how that doesn't also exempt us from doing our own part. I began to wonder, **what if God only did the minor work and then told us to do the MAJOR, ultra-demanding works?**

Well, I was born and bred in the *"Winners Family"* (Living Faith Church Worldwide/ Winners Chapel

International, *www.faithtabernacle.org.ng*), and I lived life knowing of and continuously seeing the hand of God. Well, I thought I had seen a good portion of what the hand of God could do in the lives of a people dedicated to Him but really, after the past few months, I knew that I had only seen close to nothing! In August 2015, it was announced that we, as a Church, were entering our *Wonder Double* season. This meant that at the end of October 2015, precisely October 25th 2015, we would be double our current number of Sunday worshippers.

This might sound super achievable when you think, "oh, it must be a church of maximum, 100 people. God can *maybe* do that." But instead, realise that the church we are talking about is in the Guinness Book of World Records as the largest church auditorium in the world. With a 50,000-seat capacity auditorium and 5 services already running every Sunday, one would wonder how much more people could be gathered at such a place—and then in *Otta*, Nigeria? I mean, "where exactly is that on the map," right?

Well, good thing that God doesn't listen to the worries of men when fulfilling His promises. Our faith was built as a church and my father, who is the presiding Bishop of Winners Chapel International with its headquarters in Canaanland, was unshaken in His faith. Wherever we were: at home and on the dinner table, in the car,

The Lesser Job

on a walk, *wherever*- He was completely unshaken. He was always way too confident that when God said it, He was more than able to do it. He had seen more of God than I had so far, and as we know, the more you know God, the more you know that there is to know. How awesome is it that we serve a God Who seemingly deepens in depth and *seemingly* widens in size while still remaining the same. Gosh, **what an awesome God we serve!**

Well, guess what?

We DID double in number by that Sunday! We more than doubled in number by that Sunday! On October 25th 2015, close to **500,000 people were gathered** in our *little* corner here in Nigeria and it was so sweet to SEE the fulfilment of prophecy! Even the doubters couldn't doubt anymore because now they weren't merely hearing about it, they could SEE it! Up until this day, the wonder double season continues and more people continue to be won into God's Kingdom! People go on outreaches and win tens of thousands of people to God in 8 weeks or less! How awesome God is!

God says, "bring me the chairs, I will bring in the people."

Imagine if it was the other way around and He said things like, "I'll provide the chairs but you have go out there and bring in 500,000 people to fill those seats in 'your' church by yourself and with your own power." Imagine where we would be today! Life would be way too miserable!

Instead though, He says things like, "bring me the heart, I will bring you the joy... bring me the sincerity and I will bring you the answers... bring me the truth, I will bring you salvation... bring me the truth, I will bring you freedom... **do the lesser Job, I will do the hard work.**"

He said clearly to me on that day, "I will always give you **the <u>lesser job</u>**."

He said, "**Don't try to do My job, just do yours. I'm Big enough to help Myself.**"

You cannot imagine how much freedom that brought to my heart. It was a relief and by relief, I mean that it was total. I knew from that moment on that worry is not permitted because I never have the *hard* job to do. That's God's duty and so, He will always and forever give me only, **the lesser job!**

Only a day before, I had seen God move but I knew that was only the beginning and—goodness, was that the truth!

The day before, I was with 3 of my friends in my home and we watched about a 5 minute video in which this

He will always and
forever give me only,
the lesser job!

minister of God prayed for a lady and her arms visibly grew out, causing the pains in her back to disappear. So, I asked that we measure our arms to see if anyone had a short arm. Surprisingly, one of us did!

This is the time fear should creep in because you would think "oh God, what if this doesn't grow out like I just saw?" but instead, my heart, face, and countenance emanated Joy! I loved it! I had been watching some of those videos for weeks now and had measured my limbs over and over again but they were always equal—so, this was my opportunity to VISIBLY see God at work!

She measured her arms over and over and over again just to be sure and still, they were unequal. So, I asked that she stretch her arm out and in the presence of our other two friends, prayed a short prayer and HER ARMS GREW OUT!

Oh my, to say that the room was filled with the screams of 4 humans would be an understatement. We praised God for a few minutes as we remained in complete awe! She checked her back and just like that, the pain also was gone. Pains that she had in her neck were also gone. This was super motivating, as you would imagine, so we decided to measure her legs and YES—one was shorter than the other! This was getting too exciting!

Prayed for that too and then, IT GREW OUT!

So, she checked for the knee pain that she had been having for many months and it too was GONE! Whoa!!

You know what I was thinking, right?

"Oh Lord, let her have more things that we need to grow out!" It was only the beginning of *greatness*.

I asked if she wanted her pelvis realigned as I had seen that done in those videos too and she said, "sure." So, you know what we did? I prayed a realignment prayer and just like that, the power of the Holy Spirit caused it to begin rotating and adjusting on its own. Mine and that of the other person in the room (as one of us had to leave soon after the arm growth), began rotating too! The power of God was so strong in that room and it was so undeniable. That day, was the beginning of a new journey for me.

As it was a Saturday, we had WSF (Winners Satellite Fellowship) that evening; which is a consistent Saturday meeting of the *Winners Family* in homes for one hour. As soon as it was over, those of us who had seen God move earlier in the day we were *itching* to see Him replicate some of the same miracles we had just seen. So, two of us began to ask people if they had any pains. We had predetermined that nothing would be too small or too big, to pray for. So, yes—this was so exciting!

We saw all kinds of pains healed that day and even

one woman who consistently fell under the power of God was healed of total body pains. As you can imagine, now the *thirst* was even more real!

About a week later, following our usual Saturday morning routine, a couple of friends and I went to a hospital to pray with some who were sick. I woke up that morning barely able to hear my own voice but was weirdly comfortable with it and so didn't even pray about it. I thought, this would be a *great mind your own business* tool for me today! But, on getting to the hospital, we prayed as a group for a few of the patients and as we also had two children in our group, some of us had to stay outside when it was time to go into the children's ward as kids weren't allowed in. I was one of those who stayed outside. This friend who was on the healing *frenzy* with me came out and said that she had prayed for this little girl who was in so much physical pain and couldn't lay her legs flat on the bed; she said that now, she could do so—with only "a little pain" left.

As you can imagine, my antennas went up like a flower to the sound of rain.

Woah... "a little pain?"

So I listened more as she talked and then she said this little girl had been bedridden, unable to walk for days.

As sad as this may sound to others, it was exciting to

me. This was yet another opportunity for God to show His power.

So I asked, "did you grow out her legs?" and she said no.

I mean, "ding, ding, ding...!" Yes! So I said, we would go grow out her legs.

Those who were with us, I call them the *mockers* in this instance, said to us, "why would you grow out her legs; who said they were short?"

They laughed to the point that they left us behind in the ward, but we were determined.

We went back in and merely after about two minutes praying in the Children's ward by the bedside of this little precious girl, her legs grew out; and for the first time in days, **she walked**! I will never forget her grandmother who was seated by her side and could only speak the native Nigerian Yorùbá language. She kept on thanking us and wouldn't stop but all we could say was, "Oh, that was ALL God, Ma... Just keep saying '**thank you Jesus**!'"

I mean, I know that I say and have said it over and over again but if you saw these things, I would think that you would say the same—this God is such an awesome God!

The following day, while in a short evening meeting with three others, God again caused legs to grow three times, pelvises to be rotated, and body pains to disappear. So then when one of us in the meeting said she wanted to be healed of her bow legs, what do you think we said?

Perfect but simple was our answer—"well, that's easy!"

We prayed and saw one of it straighten but gave up too easily! I know in my spirit that if we were persistent, we would have seen the complete miracle that same night but what a great God that He gives us second chances!

One would think, why pray for a bow leg?!

Well, if it hinders her from fully believing in the love of Christ because she thinks He didn't love her enough to make them straight, then He is Faithful to His Word (as always) to give His children their heart's desires. Even if it seemed cosmetic—or what YOU are believing God for now seems cosmetic—He is willing to do it for you **as long as it is in line with His Word.**

Why?

Because Psalm 23:1 (KJV) says,

"The Lord is my Shepherd, I shall not **want**."

Note that it says **want** and not **need**.

Why?

Because your needs have already been supplied

"Well, that's easy!"

according to His riches in glory (Philippians 4:19)! Now, He is asking you for what you want and not even what you need because those, you only have to demand for and as His child, you are entitled to—the enemy isn't even a factor in stopping you!

I've had times more recently when some lower back or waist pain would try to creep into my body and wherever I am, in public or private, I just whisper a prayer up to God and my pelvis begins physically rotating. Once it stops, I check my back and the pain's gone. Just the whisper puts the Holy Spirit to work! How glorious is God?!

So, **what's that one thing you've always hoped that God would do for you?**

Now, **ask** Him **in Faith**—because as long as it is in line with HIS Word (**<u>NOT yours!</u>**), then He is able, willing and ready to do it for you.

Don't let past failures *fool* you! Yes, you just read these awesome stories and may be thinking to yourself, "Oh, I wish that was me!" Well, that absolutely can be you too! –that should be you too!

The first person I ever really prayed for at a hospital died!

Yes, *she died*!

The Lesser Job

The room was so on fire that afternoon that one of us was so filled with the awe of God and eventually had to step out. In her own words, she felt like she would fall straight to the floor. Everyone was charged up and I told her entire family who was there that morning that before midnight, we would have a testimony! We took their phone numbers and everything; just to then hear that she died right around midnight.

Oh, I was so *upset* in my spirit—I thought, "little girl, I prayed for you! You should NOT have died!" but, she did. The devil would have said to himself, "finally—I've got her so she wouldn't go about praying for others." Oh, *stupid devil*—he had no idea that God was just beginning with me!

Maybe that should have stopped and deterred me but no, no, no—one *failure* isn't enough to negatively alter the course of my life! Absolutely not!

So, do not put your eyes on the things you prayed for in the past that seemingly yielded little to no result. Every day is a fresh start and an opportunity to see the hand of God in a greater dimension in your life. Remember, your job is not to do the healing or the most challenging task of the *two*. As He said to me, He will always give you, "**the lesser job**."

Your job is not to do the healing or the most challenging task of the two.... He will always give you, "the lesser job."

13

Faith Positioning

Have you ever looked at men and/or women of God who are Pastors or *Ministers* and questioned why God speaks so fluently to them but not to you? Have you ever looked at them and wondered if God loves them more than He loves you? Have you even compared yourself to friends and/or family and wondered why they alone have the *perfect* relationship with God but not you? Has that made you lose your faith in God and question whether position equals growth, love from God, and/or the faith needed to see results?

I was reading the book of Mark 5 and I saw it in a whole new light when God decided to answer these questions that I wasn't even asking. Immediately, I knew that it was for someone and yes, that someone is YOU!

Mark 5 (NIV):

> *"²¹ When Jesus had again crossed over by boat to the other side of the lake, a large crowd gathered around him while he was by the lake. ²²Then one of the synagogue leaders, named Jairus, came, and when he saw Jesus, he fell at his feet. ²³He pleaded earnestly with him, "My little daughter is dying. Please come and put your hands on <u>her so that she will be healed and live</u>." ²⁴So Jesus went with him."*

Jairus was a leader in the synagogue. He can today be equated to a pastor, bishop, or high-level administrator in the church; so, he knew *about* **the Christ**. He was a man of renown but had this one challenge and it was his daughter's health—she was very sick. As a result, he didn't care to what level his reputation would crumble if he fell at the feet of Jesus; all he knew was that Jesus could heal his daughter. So, when he gained this *easy* access (as he was a ruler and was well respected) to Jesus, he immediately fell to His feet as a sign of respect and worship. He then asked that Jesus would **come** (**NOTE**: Not that He should say a prayer or send one of His disciples but that He Himself should come); so that his daughter would be healed.

> *"A large crowd followed and pressed around him. ²⁵And a woman was there who had been subject to bleeding for twelve years. ²⁶She had*

Faith Positioning

suffered a great deal *under the care of many doctors and had* spent all *she had, yet* instead of getting better she grew worse. ²⁷When she heard *about Jesus*, she came up behind him *in the crowd* and touched his cloak, ²⁸*because she thought*, "If I just touch his clothes, I will be healed." ²⁹Immediately her bleeding stopped *and* she felt in her body that she was freed *from her suffering*."

Oh, I love this part of Scripture.

This woman didn't even have a name. Unlike the **synagogue leader**, Jairus, the Bible doesn't even tell us the name of this woman. She didn't have a title, she wasn't recognised, she didn't even have the reputation—if she did, oh my, the crowd would've made room for her just as they did for Jairus. She didn't let that stop her, though. She had this rare disease and all of town knew it because she had been to all the *good* doctors—the expensive ones who left her with absolutely no money! Oh, they did their very best but it just wasn't enough—the bleeding would NOT stop! So, she had this one last shot! She had heard about this Jesus; the One who could heal the sick and cast out unclean spirits. This was her time, finally; so, even with the bleeding and the intense weakness, she was determined. She said, "if only I can reach his clothes!" Oh, I see this great image in my head as she pushes, pulls, pants for breath and drags herself to this Jesus. She says, "I am weak, I am tired, I am bleeding... but I must make it to Jesus." So, she pulls all of herself, as best she could, to the finish line—she HAD to make it to His garment.

Oh, what a joy as soon as she could!

FINALLY, **first, by her faith,** she was healed (because if she didn't believe that she was healed after the *touch*, she would have kept dragging on Jesus' cloak). **Then,** I see the image as she immediately checks herself, with her hands on her stomach and a pause in her step (to confirm a stop in the pouring blood from the inside) and, she was healed. **Finally. Totally. Completely. She was healed.**

> "[30]At once Jesus realized that power had gone out from him. He turned around in the crowd and asked, "Who touched my clothes?" [31]"You see the people crowding against you," his disciples answered, "and yet you can ask, 'Who touched me?'" [32]But Jesus kept looking around to see who had done it. [33]Then the woman, knowing what had happened to her, came and fell at his feet and, trembling with fear, told him the whole truth. [34]He said to her, "Daughter, your faith has healed you. Go in peace and be freed from your suffering."

Our faith draws on God's power.

"I am weak, I am tired, I am bleeding... but I must make it to Jesus."

> "³⁵While Jesus was still speaking, some people came from the house of Jairus, the synagogue leader. "Your daughter is dead," they said. "Why bother the teacher anymore?"
>
> ³⁶Overhearing what they said, Jesus told him, "Don't be afraid; just believe."

Do you see that the man who was well known in the synagogue and who even was a leader needed encouragement while the woman **without a name** had so much faith that only a touch secured her healing?

> "³⁷He did not let anyone follow him except Peter, James and John the brother of James. ³⁸When they came to the home of the synagogue leader, Jesus saw a commotion, with people crying and wailing loudly. ³⁹He went in and said to them, "Why all this commotion and wailing? The child is not dead but asleep."⁴⁰But they laughed at him.
>
> After he put them all out, he took the child's father and mother and the disciples who were with him, and went in where the child was. ⁴¹He took her by the hand and said to her, "Talitha koum!" (which means "Little girl, I say to you, get up!"). ⁴²Immediately the girl stood up and began to walk around (she was twelve years old). At this they were completely astonished. ⁴³He gave strict orders not to let anyone know about this, and told them to give her something to eat."

Faith Positioning

You do not need to be a Pastor, Bishop, *well-known* Minister, or the Judge of all to see miracles. All that you need is your faith—and "...if you had faith even as small as a **mustard seed**, you could say to this mountain, 'Move from here to there,' and it would move. Nothing would be impossible" (Matthew 17:20).

Recently, and as I mentioned earlier, I began digging into understanding and seeing more of God's healing power more than ever before. So, on a certain Sunday while still in the beginning stages of this journey, I suddenly began having intense back aches as I sat in a service. I had been out for most of the day before and it was busy; filled with lots of running around and my body just wasn't used to doing all of that at one time. As I sat in the service, I thought to myself, "I know how to grow out arms but it would be *weird* stretching out my arms to do it with all these people possibly watching." So, I put my arms down by my knees and suddenly felt this pull. I looked down and lo and behold, my arm had started growing! I was surprised because I hadn't even prayed for it but God had seen my desire.

I am reminded right now of one day late after work that I prayed for this lady.

I had gotten home late after work and had another meeting to rush to in about an hour so my plan was

You do not need to be a Pastor, Bishop, well-known Minister, or the Judge of all to see miracles.

to grab dinner and rush off—honestly, I didn't think that I had even two minutes to pray with her; or so I thought. As I rushed off, she told me of how much in pain she was and even began asking what medicine I would recommend she take. So, I stopped. I rushed over to her with my massive bag in my left hand and laid my right hand on the left side of her waist. I said the prayer in my heart and literally about 10 seconds later, she said to me, "what are you doing because it feels like you're 'sucking' the pain out from my body. It's just disappearing." She then said, "you aren't even praying! What is happening?!" I said to her, "it's all the power of God" and thankfully, I got to see yet another person COMPLETELY healed in less than 30 seconds—without even praying out loud. Praise JESUS!

I say all of this to say that even though I am not a Bishop, a Pastor or a *well-known* Minister, God uses me—**and He can use YOU too**! All that He needs is your faith and willingness and you will be surprised at all that He has in store for you. As Kathryn Kuhlman once said, "[God] does not ask for golden vessels. [He] asks for yielded vessels—those who will submit their will to the will of the Father."

Only submit yourself to Him; don't aim for a position, **aim for greater faith & willingness**.

"I will put My Spirit within you and cause you to walk in My statutes, and you will be careful to observe My ordinances."
                                    Ezekiel 36:27 *(NASB)*

Salvation Prayer

We have talked so much about running to Jesus as your Saviour throughout this book and so, it is clearly important that if you are still holding on to yourself as Lord and Saviour, you surrender yourself to the Only True Lord and Saviour that there is and will ever be.

With all the faith you can muster,

Say these words out loud:

Lord Jesus,

I know that I am a sinner.

I know that I have turned my back on you repeatedly.

Today Lord, I repent of all my sins.

I believe that you died for me;

And on the third day, you rose again.

I ask that you wash me in Your Blood,

and that you take charge over my life.

Become my Lord, and lead me as my Saviour.

Now I know, that I am Born Again.

Thank you, Lord, for saving me.

Amen.

Congratulations!

Know that having said these words in faith, God has come to reside in your heart. Do not believe any more lies of the enemy and keep your focus on God. Remember, it is your responsibility to build yourself in Him. As we earlier discussed, your spirit man cannot keep saying "daada" forever. Grow in Him—start attending a Faith-based, Bible-believing church and study the Holy Bible daily—I know that from today, it will be testimony after testimony for you!

Welcome to the winning side!

www.ingramcontent.com/pod-product-compliance
Lightning Source LLC
LaVergne TN
LVHW051246080426
835513LV00016B/1764